FINDING YOUR WAY:
Seven Ways to Love & Heal Yourself

Tarnissha (Moe) Sass

Moe Sass Publishing

Allentown, PA

Finding Your Way: Seven Ways to Love and Heal Yourself

By: Tarnissha (Moe) Sass

Copyright © 2022 By Tarnissha Sass

Printed in the United States of America

ISBN: 979-8-9861200-9-6

All rights reserved. No part of this book may be reproduced or transmitted in any form, by photocopying or by any electronic or mechanical means, including information storage or retrieval systems, without permission in writing from both the copyright owner and the publisher of this book.

All Scripture quotations, unless otherwise indicated, are taken from the Holy Bible, New International Version®, NIV®. Copyright ©1973, 1978, 1984, 2011 by Biblica, Inc.™ Used by permission of Zondervan. All rights reserved worldwide. www.zondervan.com **The "NIV" and "New International Version" are trademarks registered in the United States Patent and Trademark Office by Biblica, Inc.™**

Scripture quotations marked MSG are taken from The Message, copyright © 1993, 2002, 2018 by Eugene H. Peterson. Used by permission of NavPress. All rights reserved. Represented by Tyndale House Publishers.

Scripture quotations taken from the (NASB®) New American Standard Bible®, Copyright © 1960, 1971, 1977, 1995, 2020 by The Lockman Foundation. Used by permission. All rights reserved. www.lockman.org

Internet addresses (websites, blogs, public figure mentions, etc.) printed in this book are offered as a resource to you. These are not intended in any way to imply endorsement on the part of Moe Sass Publishing, nor do we vouch for the content of these sites for the life of this book.

Acknowledgments

I'd like to say thank you to:

- ✓ God for EVERYTHING that I am and growing to become.

- ✓ My grandmother, Josephine Sass, whose prayers are the reason this book is completed.

- ✓ My grandmother, Virginia Blackwell, whose strength kept me.

- ✓ My Aunt Gina, who reminded me not to drop the ball.

- ✓ My children, Sahaad, Ashley, Antwoine, Alexus, Kamurah and Kamren, who push me to be the best me.

- ✓ All my ancestors, who love me and continue to hold me up throughout my journey.

- ✓ Kuseem Chandler, for inspiring me through his literary work to put pen to paper.

Table Of Contents

Introduction vii

Chapter 1

    No One Wins When The Family Feuds 1

Chapter 2

    Change Your Vocabulary,
    Transform Your Life 11

Chapter 3

    Move Your Body and Free Your Mind 19

Chapter 4

    If It's White, It's Not Right.
    If It's Brown, Lay It Down. 27

Chapter 5
   Without Vision, the People Perish............41

Chapter 6
   Proper Preparation Prevents Poor Performance..55

Chapter 7
   Who Holds You Accountable?............67

Conclusion............75

Let's Connect............79

About the Author............81

Introduction

*Grow a wise heart—you'll do yourself a favor;
keep a clear head-you'll find a good life.*
Proverbs 19:8 (MSG)

One night I looked up after yet another failed relationship and said enough was enough. I knew there was more to life than all that I had been experiencing. I had friendships that fell apart—I mean people I loved deeply. I don't let people into my heart easily, so if someone could feel my heart, I gave it ALL away. I was burnt out. I was exhausted. I always over-gave, over-committed, over-cared, over-cried, and I was OVER IT!

I didn't realize that what I was seeking was also seeking me, but not in the way that I "thought." Thoughts were one of my biggest issues because I "thought" people would love me, show up and care for me like I cared for them. I believed if I did everything, people would somehow "know" to do the same for me. Keywords: thought and know. My thoughts were the things that kept me trapped because I was an overthinker. I could make a situation better or worse in my mind than it actually was, which meant I could accept less in my life because I always made excuses for everyone's behavior, including mine. I told myself I was a nice person, loved extremely hard, and had to give people the benefit of the doubt because I didn't want them to think I thought I was better than them.

Growing up, I would hear family members say that I thought I was better than others. Meanwhile, I hated myself. I thought my nose was too big; I looked like a man; my butt was too big; I was too dark and wasn't lovable. Since those were my beliefs, I did everything in my power to live up to them. I cowered down, shrunk myself, and hid the fullness of who I was to fit into a narrative of people who had no idea what I felt about myself.

I started by saying, what I was seeking, was seeking me. I was seeking love in ALL the WRONG places; therefore, that was seeking me. All the wrong people, places and things were posing as love but were very toxic.

Then the revelation came—there had to be more than this. I was tired of crying over failed relationships and friendships. I was tired of being criticized for who I was, the way I thought and how I felt. See, I'm a dreamer. I have a vision that some may think is a bit fairytale-ish and naïve. But, I finally understood after my last relationship they were right all along. I am a dreamer, visionary, out-of-the-box thinker, hopeless romantic and timeless; it's just that I was with the wrong people.

I was expecting people to give me what I hadn't given myself. That's why I didn't recognize the dream killers for who they were. I want to state that I don't think any of the people who have come and gone from my life are bad people. As a matter of fact, I love them to death. Why? Because of them, I found

ME! They helped me kill off the old, outdated parts of me that needed to be validated, chosen and seen that lived in a lack mentality. Because of them, I love the HELL OUT OF ME. Because of them, I am now in the right rooms. Because of them, I chose. Because of them, I validate myself. Because of them, my death and rebirth have transformed me into the most beautiful butterfly. Because of them, I know that God, my angels and my ancestors have never left me. Because of them, I dedicate this book to the greatest love of all: self-love.

Now it's your turn.

> *When you learn to love yourself, it trickles down for generations. We make generations of healed people instead of hurt people.*

The seven principles listed in this book will help you begin inner reflection that will lead to your healing. Each chapter will provide journal prompts and mirror affirmations to help you dig deeper. Take your time as you go through this book. Set aside a time and place where you won't be interrupted.

Here is why affirmations are important: "Affirmation" is defined as the action or process of affirming or being affirmed; emotional support or encouragement. Affirmations are important because faith comes by hearing. Once you start to affirm yourself, it will help you believe in yourself and erase those doubts and fears about who you are that linger in the back of your mind.

I want to teach you how to validate yourself internally and externally through affirmations. The way to do this is to look in the mirror and say, "I AM _____," and then validate it by saying, "YES, YOU ARE_____." In all my years of teaching fitness and life coaching, I discovered that speaking life into yourself in a convicting way helps affirm the words as if they are true. It also helps you affirm yourself. Many people search outside themselves for validation, but NOT YOU, NOT EVER AGAIN! A major key is to do your affirmations every day. Why? Repetition is mastery. Think about when you learned multiplication in school. You had to go over the facts and figures daily to engrain 12 x 12 = 144 in your mind. That's how affirmations work. You say them repeatedly until you believe with conviction that it is who you are. Then, you will begin to validate yourself and no longer seek the approval of others.

As you dig deeper by answering the journal prompts, I hope this book opens you up to your healing journey of self-love. Everywhere we turn, we hear the term self-love, but there are many interpretations without real context. Self-love is more than taking a candlelit bubble bath or spa day. Self-love is about taking accountability for your life. It's an understanding that all things begin and end with you. If you make a declaration to stand in your power and own your life, accepting everything there is about what's happening in you and around you, that's self-love. Self-love is standing in your power. Self-love is accepting all parts of you while working to heal and remove the things that no longer serve your highest good.

The healing process involves the death of old parts of yourself. While I want to say that the journey is all rainbows and sunshine, it's not true. Just as in any death, there is a grieving process. There are no rainbows without rain. It can be tough to face the parts of yourself that hold any limiting beliefs, fears, traumas and thoughts of lack. As tough as it may be at times, that's what self-love is. It's saying I love myself enough to face mental, emotional, physical, nutritional, or spiritual disconnects in my life. I use the term disconnect because I want to get away from the stigma of "brokenness." We are not broken. Many people have trauma from early childhood that causes an internal disconnect. This could have disconnected you from your authentic, loving self. Disconnected you from your innocence. Disconnected you from your emotions. Most people have no idea what they are feeling, let alone being able to express it in a way that's not hurtful and harmful. A part of loving yourself is facing the disconnect so you can live an abundant life of health, wealth, and love.

Here are some things to ponder as you read each chapter:

If you can't be real, you can't be healed. ~ Sanctuary

What will you say yes to today?

As I think, so I feel.

As I feel, so I do.

As I do, so I have.

> *I have always grown from my problems and challenges, from the things that don't work out; that's when I've really learned.*
> *Carol Burnett*

CHAPTER 1

No One Wins When The Family Feuds

God has called us to live in peace.
1 Corinthians 7:15 (NIV)

"Nobody wins when the family feuds" is a lyric coined by rapper Jay-Z in the song "Family Feud" from the *444* Album. One premise of the song dealt with the state of America at the time, but there was an aspect of the song where Jay-Z used his personal life as a lesson when he stated, "A house divided against itself cannot stand." What I loved about the song's ultimate message was that

Jay-Z clarified that the family feud didn't just consist of conflict between his wife and outside individuals. The family feud was about him being at war within himself. As a result of him conflicting with himself, he was ultimately dividing his family because when you wrestle with the inner conflicts, you begin consciously or sometimes unconsciously declaring war on those sent to love you. In the song, Jay-Z talked about how he wasn't committed to complaining about the problem. Instead, He realized that he was the problem and sought therapy for his toxic traits, including infidelity, dishonesty, and lack of accountability. That started to make me think about how many families could be saved if we took accountability for the family feud happening inside of each of us. The feud between head, heart and soul.

If you're at odds with yourself and don't love yourself, then no one around you wins. You lose because you don't have internal peace if you're always at odds with how you look, feel, express yourself and think. Therefore, coming into mental, emotional, physical, financial and spiritual alignment is essential on your journey to loving you.

Webster's Dictionary defines alignment as the state of being arranged in a line or proper position. When you're aligned mentally, emotionally, physically, nutritionally, and financially, it positions you not to be in survival mode. Conversely, it's impossible to thrive in life when you're out of alignment.

Alignment is matching your thoughts, words, and actions. For example, if you say you'll write a book, but don't think you're smart enough, so you don't write it, none of that matches. Coming into alignment means understanding your gift is too valuable not to share. Writing a book is a process you're capable of, and as a result, you write for 20 minutes daily. Twenty minutes a day doesn't seem like a lot; however, 20 minutes a day for 365 days is 7,300 minutes. Not to say that the process takes that long, but this example demonstrates that small daily actions lead to big wins and a finished book.

Another example would be saying you love yourself but hate what you see when you look in the mirror. Or, every time you want to say no to something or someone, you say yes, and resent it later. Coming into alignment would be looking in the mirror, loving all of who you are, and only making adjustments if you want to be a healthier version of yourself. Also, setting boundaries with people is part of coming into alignment. No is a complete sentence, and saying no will allow you to do the things that bring you happiness instead of resentment.

Being a mother, wife, friend, husband, boyfriend, girlfriend, or partner does not mean sacrificing all of yourself for them. Learning to come into alignment and taking care of yourself first will allow you to be the best in someone else's life. Loving yourself isn't selfish; it's selfless. When you're the best you, then you show up in a much healthier and happier way. You'll be fun to be around. When you're resentful, burnt out, stressed out, exhausted, and lacking self-love, no one wants to be around that. The energy reeks of misery. It not only drains you, but you become a drain to everyone around you. Just because people don't express it to you doesn't make it untrue. Also, some people may express it to you, but because you're not in alignment, you get defensive and turn it around on them. As a result, they don't want to communicate with you about anything else. Alignment is a bridge to freedom because you will no longer betray yourself.

Once you decide to take control of your life and get into alignment, start by taking an internal inventory of where you don't feel whole. A way to take inventory is by journaling. You can't change what you don't acknowledge or pretend not to know, so write down everything you aren't happy about in your life.

If you're reading this book, there's no room to live in denial about what's happening in and around you any longer. You are the CEO of your life. That means it's time to stop running the business of you into the ground and handle the business. Look at every area of your life and note what you don't like and why you don't like it. This can't be a surface exercise. If you want freedom from repeating patterns of unhappiness in your life, it's time to dig deep.

Here are some journal questions to help you dig deeper. Write in your journal daily and reflect on where you may be mentally, emotionally, physically, nutritionally, and financially out of alignment.

***

If you're complaining without taking action, YOU are choosing to stay committed to complaining and not changing. This drains not only you but those around you too.

Question: What's the one thing you complain about the most that you're committed to changing, and how will you measure that?

_____

_____

_____

_____

_____

_____

***

At the beginning of the chapter, I gave an example of some of Jay-Z's toxic traits. The truth is we all have toxic traits, and when you identify and call them forth, you can work on them. You can't do the same things and expect a different outcome in your life. You can't be authentic if you tell the same lie to yourself and others, which places you out of alignment with who you truly are.

Question: What's the one toxic trait that you're committed to changing?

_____

_____

_____

_____

_____

_____

***

Action creates momentum. Small steps every day lead to big changes. We're no longer tossing around the word self-love; we're going to live it. In other words, don't talk about it; be about it.

Question: What's the one small step you can take today to love yourself enough to get aligned mentally, physically, emotionally, nutritionally, or spiritually? You can choose one or more, but don't choose more than two to avoid overwhelming yourself.

_____

_____

_____

_____

_____

_____

***

If you don't acknowledge where you consistently betray yourself, you'll continue to resent yourself and others. It's one thing to identify toxic traits, but more often, I've found that people will put others before their own well-being.

Question: In what areas of your life are you saying yes when you want to say no?

_____
_____
_____
_____
_____
_____
_____

***

Surrendering to inner peace by stopping the feud within yourself will set you on the course to become a better you and make everyone around you better as you love yourself enough to become aligned. Here are the mirror affirmations for you to practice daily. Say them aloud at least three times each. In the beginning of the book, I expressed the importance of Affirmations and why reaffirming yourself is important. Validating yourself is key along this journey.

Mirror Affirmations:

Affirm	Reaffirm
I am in tune with my intuition.	You are in tune with your intuition.
I am emotionally intelligent.	You are emotionally intelligent.
I am fearless.	You are fearless.
I am leading with love.	You are leading with love.

We plant seed that will flower as
results in our lives, so best to remove
the weeds of anger, avarice, envy,
and doubt, that peace and abundance
may manifest for all.
Dorothy Day

CHAPTER 2

Change Your Vocabulary, Transform Your Life

*A gentle answer turns away wrath,
but a harsh word stirs up anger.*
Proverbs 15:1 (NIV)

Life and death are in the tongue. That means whatever you speak shall be. This is not just a random cliché. Think about all the times you have spoken things into existence, negative or positive. Most people don't realize all of their limiting language.

I didn't realize how my language was killing the very things I loved. As a life coach, I thought I had it all together until the day my relationship fell apart. I couldn't understand what went wrong until I started my therapy sessions, where I realized that I had a limiting belief around relationships. During my relationships, I would say that it wouldn't last, or I was fine being by myself. I said it jokingly sometimes, but I wasn't always joking.

I wasn't saying I was fine by myself to prove that I wasn't afraid of being alone. I was saying it from a place of feeling like I could do without ever having a relationship. The problem with the statement was that it wasn't how I felt. I was in love, but instead of speaking love, I spoke as if the relationship didn't matter to me. If you haven't guessed already, my relationship ended. There were many contributing factors, but it didn't help that I spoke death over it and wasn't in alignment.

I want to add a disclaimer here: I firmly believe you must be okay with being alone, and you shouldn't enter a relationship because you're lonely. I believe you must be happy with yourself inside and out, with or without a relationship. The point I'm making is this: Don't speak ill or nonchalantly over something that you love—mainly YOU.

When you speak death (negatively) over yourself or someone else, it's from a place of fear. If you're talking negatively about yourself, what do you fear about the positive side? Or why don't you see a positive side? Can you pinpoint when you began to start feeling and talking that way? We can't make things better until we stop making things worse. You have to identify the root of where it all began and why. How do you speak about yourself? Be honest! If you have ever said or thought any of the following, write it down: I'm stupid; I'm dumb; I should have known better; I'm a failure; I'm not enough; I don't have enough; I'm not good enough; I can't communicate; it's impossible; I don't understand; I'm not smart enough; I can't figure it out; they know more than me; I'm crazy; I'm going to sound crazy, etc.

Do you notice a pattern in these words?

I don't; I am; I'm not; I can't; impossible.

Here's what I want you to know:

When you say I don't, you won't.

When you say I am, you are.

When you say I'm not, you're not.

When you say I can't, you won't.

When you say impossible, it will never be possible.

By limiting your vocabulary to those negative words, you're limiting your beliefs and actions. This creates a never-ending story of lack.

It's time to change your vocabulary, and it starts by adding small daily habits of replacing what I call death terms. I define death terms as any words that can kill your mind, spirit, hopes and dreams. Replace death terms with life terms that light you on fire with passion, purpose, hope and love. As you're working on this, the first thing to do is pause before you speak or respond. This will allow you to gather your words and thoughts. This is important because your language introduces you as soon as you open your mouth. Practicing your affirmations like the ones at the end of the chapter in the mirror or just saying them aloud as often as possible will help transform your vocabulary.

Here are some journal questions to help you dig deeper. Write in your journal daily and reflect on where you have written any of the death terms. Then, cross them out and replace them with life terms to help shape better habits.

***

I want to start by helping you identify some unconscious patterns. We're often playing a never-ending story in our heads that keeps us in a negative space about ourselves. This could be something that happened as an adolescent or adult. For example, blaming yourself for a breakup and then considering yourself unworthy of the love you truly desire.

Question: What never-ending story are you telling yourself?

_____

_____

_____

_____

_____

_____

***

To truly see yourself after answering the question below, try to identify where in your life you may be sabotaging yourself unintentionally.

Question: What are some negative statements you say daily, and how are they holding you back?

_____

_____

_____

_____

_____

_____

***

Do you need additional resources such as a therapist, life coach or mentor? Asking for help is essential on your journey. The following questions are to reflect on getting to the root and determining if you need help to uncover, heal and transform negativity to positivity.

Question: In what areas of your life does the negative talk show up the most?

_____

_____

_____

_____

_____

_____

Question: Where do the negative words that you speak come from? When was the first time you heard and started to believe them?

_____

_____

_____

_____

_____

_____

***

It's time to practice your mirror affirmations: Be sure to write them down and place them where you can see them often. You can use sticky notes or put them on the home screen of your phone. You want to be sure to speak them a minimum of three times daily.

Mirror Affirmations:

Affirm	Reaffirm
I am powerful.	You are powerful.
I am positive.	You are positive.
I can be, do or have anything I set my mind to.	You can be, do or have anything you set your mind to.
I am brilliant.	You are brilliant.
I am successful.	You are successful.

Don't forget that a single sentence, spoken at the right moment, can change somebody's whole perspective on life. A little encouragement can go a long way.
Marie T. Freemon

CHAPTER 3

Move Your Body and Free Your Mind

Didn't you realize that your body is a sacred place, the place of the Holy Spirit? Don't you see that you can't live however you please, squandering what God paid such a high price for?
1 Corinthians 6:19 (MSG)

Disclaimer: *Please check with your physician before starting any fitness regimen.*

Fitness saved me. I wasn't diagnosed with an illness by any doctor; I was battling life. December 11, 2010, at around 2:00 a.m., my phone rang, and my life was NEVER the same after that call. I immediately jumped out of bed and told my now ex-husband, "I got to go," and he proceeded to question me. I didn't have time for his questions, but I knew he needed answers. I said, "He's been shot," and although my ex had just had surgery on his neck to remove a lump and could barely move, he got up and proceeded out the door with me.

Later we would find out that our oldest son, who was 25 years old, was shot in the chest. It rocked our entire family. We had a total of six kids. Three girls and three boys. Now we had to return home to tell them they no longer had an older brother. My ex-husband and I also had to face the reality of burying our second son. In 1998 after going into labor at six months, our son, Kenneth Allen McCoy, took one breath and passed away. Not to mention our marriage had been on the rocks for years before our eldest's death. We finally divorced in 2011. It was a tailspin of emotions.

Whether I was depressed, stressed, or broke, going

to the gym for a minimum of one hour a day, six days a week, helped get me through it all. At first, I was just working out, but in 2010, I became certified to teach fitness just six days before our son's murder.

After long days of being at home with my four younger kids, who were consistently sad because of their brother's death, I would prepare myself to teach in the gym. My then-husband was depressed after chemotherapy and radiation treatments. We discovered he had stage three cancer the same week our son was murdered. Bills were piling up, and I had no clue what I was feeling because I was too busy caring for my family.

After all of that, I gave my all when I walked into the gym to teach. For one hour, I was free from the pain, guilt, kids, bills and stress that had overtaken my life. For one hour, I danced, cried, smiled and laughed with the people in my fitness class. As it turned out, they were battling life too. They shared their stories and told me that coming to class saved them. For that one hour, the fitness class was happiness, joy, and everything I needed just to breathe. I'm standing tall today because I loved myself enough to go to one of my therapeutic outlets, which was my passion and purpose—the gym.

Physical fitness is not about losing weight in the world of self-love. I describe physical fitness in this setting as a form of therapy. I want to state that physical fitness in NO WAY replaces a therapist, but it can help free your mind and soul from the punches life throws at you. Also, my statements here are not meant to be an inspiration or motivation to get you to join a gym. Motivation and inspiration are temporary. I don't want to motivate you for a minute. My hope is what you read in this book will transform you for a lifetime, but a gym membership isn't required.

Some benefits that you gain from working out are letting out frustration, gaining clarity and focus, reducing stress, and discovering energy to stay in the fight of life. Health is wealth, and to obtain and maintain wealth, you must develop healthy habits in your life.

The key is to make it FUN! Try many different types of fitness until you find the one thing you have the most fun doing. Dance fitness, weight training and kickboxing were classes that I loved, but I worked out at home for years before joining a gym. You DO NOT need a gym. There are many free programs on YouTube and on-demand programs like Beachbody and Les Mills. Joining a gym is great for being part of a community, and when you want to transform your life, getting into a community of like-minded individuals will help you. I found some of my greatest friends and accountability partners while going to the gym, and an instructor who saw me light up in her class introduced me to the idea of teaching. You never know what you will find when you step out of your comfort zone and enter the fitness zone. Set yourself up to become the best YOU that you can be by allowing fitness to be a part of your therapy. If you're interested in joining my free community, email me at info@moesass.com.

Here are some journal questions to help you dig deeper. As I stated earlier, we can't make things better until we stop making things worse, so take some time and journal the answers to these questions.

***

Let's begin by identifying obstacles and what stands in your way of setting a schedule.

Question: What stands in the way of you moving your body daily, even walking?

_____

_____

_____

_____

_____

We all have battles that we face in life. Building a healthy lifestyle helps build your mental strength to handle life's many challenges.

Question: How can you give yourself one hour? If not an hour, reserve 20, 30, or 45 minutes of whatever time you can to set your mind free, relieve stress and gain focus by moving your body.

_____

_____

_____

_____
_____

_____

Question: How can you make a schedule that ensures you develop a routine that includes moving your body at least five days a week?

_____

_____
_____
_____
_____
_____

Question: Are you willing to join a community of like-minded individuals to help you succeed?

_____
_____
_____
_____
_____

***

It's time to practice your mirror affirmations: Be sure to write them down and place them where you can see them often. You can use sticky notes or put them on the home screen of your phone. You want to be sure to speak them a minimum of three times daily.

Mirror Affirmations:

Affirm	Reaffirm
I love my body.	Your body is beautiful.
I am strong.	You are strong.
I am a winner.	You are a winner.
I am focused.	You are focused.
I am physically fit.	You are physically fit.

Mind and body in harmony
provide all the necessary strength for
happy, healthy living
Charmaine Saunders

CHAPTER 4

If It's White, It's Not Right. If It's Brown, Lay It Down.

*It is not good to eat too much honey,
nor is it honorable to search out matters
that are too deep.
Proverbs 25:27*

Disclaimer: *I am not a licensed nutritionist. Please check with your physician before starting any dietary lifestyle changes.*

The body is made in the kitchen, NOT the gym. What you feed your body is an intricate part of loving yourself. We live in a fast-paced, fast-food society that essentially sells us garbage posing as food. We're eating products high in sodium, sugar and saturated fats. My philosophy is garbage in your mouth, garbage out. The garbage out can be diabetes, which according to the Centers for Disease Control and Prevention (CDC), affects 463 million adults worldwide. In the U.S. alone, 34.2 million people have diabetes. That's 10.5% of the American population. The garbage out can also be hypertension. According to the CDC, 47% of adults in the U.S. (116 million) have hypertension.

Do you love yourself enough to eat clean? I live by an 80/20 rule. Eighty percent of the time, I eat clean; twenty percent of the time, I allow the enjoyment of life. When I refer to eating clean, that means if the food dies quickly, you should eat that 80% of the time. What foods die quickly? Fresh fruits, vegetables and meat (if you eat meat). Food that doesn't die quickly includes items with a long shelf life, like pasta and canned goods.

When it comes to the latest diet trends, I don't subscribe to them. The first three letters in the word diet are DIE. I don't speak death in anything that I do. I'm about lifestyle changes. What that means is if you're not going to follow a diet trend at 70, don't do it now. When you think about a lifestyle change, this is something that you can maintain regardless of age. You can eat foods with less saturated fat, sugar, and salt and drink water for the rest of your life. I like to keep it simple. I'm not knocking fad diets, i.e., Keto, SlimFast, etc., because I understand that people may use them to jumpstart their new lifestyle. However, I want to be clear that they are not sustainable for a lifetime.

If it's white, it's not right, and if it's brown, lay it down: Start slowly by replacing all white products with brown ones. For example, no white, sugar, bread, or pasta. Instead, replace them with whole-grain bread and pasta. If extra sugar is required, it's better to use organic cane sugar. The goal is to eliminate as much additive sugar as possible. Most people don't realize there's sugar in everything. Start looking at the backs of all the sauces you eat—they're loaded with sugar.

Sugar is just as addictive as drugs and alcohol. I know this seems like a stretch, but try kicking the habit and going without sugar. Also, according to a 2018 review by PubMed Central, the most common foods associated with addictive symptoms are those high in added fats or SUGAR.

I went on a sugar detox. Some initial side effects were cravings, lightheadedness, headaches, body cramps, anxiety, anger and low energy until the symptoms subsided, which took almost two weeks. Ironically, after cutting out sugar for 45 days, I had clearer skin, more energy, and fewer mood swings. I lost weight because my appetite decreased when my sugar cravings waned. Overall, I just felt better. Please note that I was under the care of a health professional, and I don't recommend doing a cold-turkey detox or fast.

If it's loaded with salt, it's time to halt: Too much salt can lead to hypertension and water retention. Instead of salt, try seasonings like Mrs. Dash, Flavor Gods, and any other natural salt-free seasoning.

Carb Control: When you think of carbs, avoid simple carbs such as potato chips, white bread, white sugar, and white pasta. Eat more complex carbs like sweet potatoes, cauliflower rice, brown rice and whole-grain or vegetable pasta. Complex carbs pack in more nutrition, are higher in fiber, digest slower, and are more filling, which is great for weight control. Complex carbs are ideal for Type-2 diabetic patients because they help manage blood sugar spikes after meals.

Plate portions: All your food should fit in the center of the plate and not spill off the sides. Half the plate should be vegetables: spinach, greens, etc.; a six-ounce protein (if you eat meat), and four to six ounces of a complex carbohydrate. A way to measure six ounces is if the cooked meat is about the size of the palm of your hand.

Hydration: Replace all your drinks with water. Before you throw the book across the room, coffee drinkers, I'm not telling you to give up your best part of waking up. I'm saying you should drink water for the rest of the day. You can flavor up the water with MIO, Crystal Light and fresh fruit until you get used to plain, spring or alkaline water.

Dairy: If you want to cut down on congestion and inflammation, then cut the dairy. If you consume too much lactose, it can inflame your large intestine, and diarrhea can develop. Dairy products are mucus-forming, and the protein in dairy increases inflammation in vital body parts, such as the thyroid gland and digestive tract. When you think about mucus forming, this is why when you develop a cold or flu, doctors will tell you to cut out dairy and replace it with Vitamin C, also known as orange juice. The inflammation caused by dairy may also promote the growth of unhealthy gut bacteria linked to chronic conditions such as leaky gut. Many people were raised on dairy, and it may seem hard to give up, but there are many options for milk substitution, such as almond and coconut milk. There are ice cream substitutions like Halo Top or So Delicious almond milk ice cream. There are also a wide variety of non-dairy creamers. When I cut dairy from my diet and my kids' diets, we all stopped getting sick as much in the winter months and had less inflammation. With that being said, please remember to consult a physician before cutting any food group.

A rule of thumb: If it's in the house, it's in the mouth. Please don't fool yourself into believing that you can purchase a bunch of unhealthy snacks, sugary drinks and ice cream and not be tempted to eat them. I'm not telling you to throw it all away; I'm telling you to become aware of what you are consuming in your body. Awareness is key, and moderation will lead to success. It's not that you can never indulge; it's about indulging in moderation. For example, when I go out to dinner, I enjoy whatever food and drink I desire. It teaches your mind and body that those foods are a treat, not for daily consumption. This allows you to enjoy life yet remain as healthy as possible.

Do you love yourself enough to take the time out to cook and feed your body good foods? Buying organic food isn't more expensive; it takes proper planning by looking at ads to know when things are on sale. Here is my theory on expenses – it's all relative. I was on welfare, getting $322 a month as a teen mom, and I still purchased $100 shoes. That was irresponsible, but that's not the point I'm making. The point I'm making is that we spend money on the things we want. Now is the time to spend money on things we need. We need to feed our bodies healthy food. We need to feed our children and spouses healthy food. It may feel expensive temporarily, but when you think long-term about the lack of health issues you will have, then it's worth it. This begins with you loving yourself enough to be the leader in your household in health and wellness.

If you're a parent, I know you think this won't work in your home. I'm here to tell you that I did all the above in my household, and at first, my kids were resistant, but they got used to it. Here's the best part: I don't get sick as much as I used to, and my kids don't, either. No more colds, congestion, or flu. They became less sluggish in their sports.

I stopped buying sugary drinks altogether when my kids played sports because I had a travel cheerleader, a softball player and a baseball player. I would buy them Gatorade for practices and game day only. I also had two children diagnosed with ADHD, and when I removed the dyes and sugar from their diets, they could focus better, so it was a blessing they never had to take any prescription medications.

In addition to changing my kids' diets, I also

took away screen time, which changed their lives. My daughter, who I was told would never be in a normal class or go to college, was taking honors classes in high school, and she graduated from college with a bachelor's degree in Criminal Justice. I know not all cases are the same, and there is no shame if a child needs medication or educational assistance, but I wanted to share some of the holistic methods I used to help my family succeed.

Here are some journal questions to help you dig deeper in your nutrition journey.

***

It's important to determine why and when you eat. For example, are you an emotional eater? Reflecting on this will help you form healthier habits. After you determine the when and the why, next, I want you to think about healthy substitutions.

Question: When do you find that you eat the most?

_____

_____

_____

_____

_____

_____

_____

***

Now it's time to assess if you have any limiting beliefs around finances or lack of control. A limiting belief is a state of mind or belief about yourself that restricts you in some way. These beliefs don't always have to be about yourself, either. They could be about how you interact with people, ideas, and how the world works. For example, if you find yourself thinking things like, *I'm not strong enough to resist eating fast food; I'm just not good with money; money is the root of all evil,* or *I don't have time,* these are limiting beliefs. They stop you from progressing and hold you back from achieving your goals. To overcome any limiting beliefs, we must identify the statements that we consistently make so we can break the cycle. Again, we can't change what we don't acknowledge.

Question: What are your beliefs about purchasing and eating organic food?

_____

_____

_____

_____

_____

_____

_____

_____

***

I want you to think about food from a different perspective. This may seem harsh, but keep an open mind and think about this. Could you imagine after your final days on earth, if your tombstone read, "Here lies (insert your name) who died because of overindulging with saturated fat, salt, and sugar"? When you think about how that sounds, it helps put things into perspective.

Question: What do you want the words on your tombstone to read?

_____

_____

_____

_____

_____

_____

_____

Question: If you're unsure of the right foods to eat, who can you reach out to for support?

_____

_____

_____

_____

_____

_____

_____

***

It's time to practice your mirror affirmations: Be sure to write them down and place them where you can see them often. You can use sticky notes or put them on the home screen of your phone. You want to be sure to speak them a minimum of three times daily.

Mirror Affirmations:

Affirm	Reaffirm
I am healthy.	You are healthy.
I love eating healthy.	You are eating healthy.
I feel amazing.	You are amazing.
I am worthy.	You are worthy.
I am a great cook.	You are the best cook.

Exercise is king. Nutrition is queen. Put them together and you've got a kingdom.

Jack LaLanne

CHAPTER 5

Without Vision, the People Perish

*Do not neglect the spiritual
gift within you
1 Timothy 4:14 (NASB)*

There's a song by the rapper Drake entitled "Fancy." The lyrics go like this: "Oh, you fancy, huh? Nails done, hair done, everything did." It was a huge summer anthem because it was about women who made sure they were put together head to toe before they stepped out. I must have been in the mirror getting dressed to that song many nights because it solidified how I felt about the way I was looking heading out of the house.

I'm ALL for looking fancy; as a matter of fact, it's my guilty pleasure to get all dressed up and go out. While that's a pleasure, it's only about what's on the surface. I want us to get to a place where our inner person is as fancy as our outer appearance. We have a saying in my community: Ugly inside, ugly outside. That means I don't care how much you work on your outer appearance; if your heart, mind, and soul are ugly, so are you. Most people plan to take care of their external image to look picture perfect but don't have an actual vision for their life and are internally empty. They plan their hair and nails appointments and go to the mall but don't have a plan for their mental, emotional, spiritual, family, and financial life.

A vision is defined as the ability to think about or plan the future with imagination or wisdom. A vision is important because when you know where you're headed, you can't get distracted and pulled off course. God said to write the vision and make it plain. That means making it as simple as cutting out pictures, placing them on a vision board and writing the vision on paper. Faith comes by hearing, and when you speak your vision daily, it helps increase your faith. Therefore, you want to make it visible so you can see it daily. A vision is not one-dimensional. You want to create a vision for your family, health, finances, and career. What do you want for your family? What do you want for your marriage (if you desire partnership)? What do you want for your finances?

Have you ever been in a relationship and looked over at your partner and thought, "How did I end up here?" It's because you didn't have a clear vision for the type of relationship you desired and the character traits of the person with whom you wanted to enter into a relationship. When you're happy with being chosen instead of knowing that you chose your life partner, resentment, fear, anger and dissatisfaction lead to the breakup.

Imagine you have a vision for how you desire to feel in the relationship. You envision your partner being authentic, spiritually obedient, financially stable, vulnerable, emotionally available, and living in their divine purpose. When someone comes along and you begin to get to know them, but they don't have any of the characteristics in your vision, you know they're not the person for you. I want you to notice the character traits that I used. They don't say 6'5" tall, short hair, dark-skinned, or any other physical features. I'm not saying you shouldn't be physically attracted to a partner, but you should measure a person by their character, not their looks. If you look and smell good but lack integrity, how does that work? If integrity is a part of your vision, it will help you not settle for people you already know won't work for you.

When I didn't have a vision for my finances and love life, I veered off-track in some bad relationships. I ended up giving away and spending more money than I had to spend. I gave money to people who never intended to pay it all back. What I was doing was putting my family in a financial bind. I grew up believing you should give a person the shirt off your back, so I was robbing Peter to pay Paul. It wasn't that I didn't have the means, but I loaned or gave money to others without a thought about what it would cost my family. I didn't know to have a vision for my finances. But now, my household comes first, and my vision states how much I plan to live off of, save, invest, and earn over the next few years.

I want to be clear that I still believe in giving; however, now that I have a financial vision, giving will never come at the cost of my family's security. The same goes for my love life. I didn't have a vision for the type of man I wanted, so I accepted behaviors no person should. I found myself in relationships with men who cheated multiple times, endured physical and mental abuse, and loaned money I never received back. I took on their burdens as if they were mine, helping to take care of their children, bills, and mental health issues while neglecting myself.

I remember it like yesterday, in the relationship after my divorce. I didn't even know what it was to love myself, let alone have a vision. I was standing in the mirror, cleaning up my bruises because this was the worst it had ever gotten. He had been angry before, and admittedly, I had hit him before, BUT never had it been this bad. I knew I needed to go to the doctor, but I was too embarrassed to go around where I lived. I was already embarrassed enough because this was the first time anyone would see what was a secret behind closed doors. The night before, we were outside in front of my house, and his fists were flying while I was on the ground trying to cover myself. My neighbors a few houses down were screaming, "Get off of her!" I couldn't believe it was all happening. They called the cops, he fled, and what did I do? I tried to lie. I was more worried about the cops arresting him than the fact that my ear was ringing—I couldn't hear out my left ear—my mouth was bleeding, my head was swelling, and my ribs were aching. The saddest part of all is, I thought I deserved it because I had hurt people in my past and thought this was "karma" coming for her payback. I didn't think I was worthy and subconsciously thought it was normal to fight in a relationship. I would end up going back to him and eventually having a marriage ceremony that would last three months before I had the courage to completely walk away never to speak or see him again. I declared from that moment on that I would NEVER be in that type of relationship ever again. That was when I learned through seeking therapy to start loving myself and gaining a clear vision for who and what I wanted in my life. I know some will read this and judge, and that's okay. I was merely surviving. Creating a vision for every aspect of my life moved me from surviving to writing my story and thriving.

This leads me to the most important vision of them all. Every person should have this vision because it will take you to the next level of your life—a spiritual vision. I am spiritual, not religious. That means I have a personal relationship with God. I read, write, and meditate (pray) daily. I will never tell anyone what or who they should call their God. It's important to understand that having a higher power in your life will make a difference and create a life of abundance in all things. When I went through life's battles, my friends, ex-husband and family couldn't help me. It was God and me! It's because of God that I've written this book.

I understand that when people discuss Spirituality, it can be off-putting because of how "humans" have abused and misused God's name to serve their selfish purposes. I apologize to anyone coming across my book who has had that experience. I was brought up under religious guidelines and understand them all too well. I would hear things such as, "Children are to be seen not heard; spare the rod, spoil the child; never question an adult." While words alone didn't hurt, the humans who chose to use them to abuse others like myself made them hurt.

When I was sexually touched at age 13 by my aunt's boyfriend, what I discovered as an adult in my spiritual healing journey is humans have FREE WILL. Free will to harm, hurt, steal from, abuse and misuse others. I don't believe God has ever, nor will ever, allow abuse. Even though I was harmed as a child, God has kept and saved me despite other's abusive ways and lack of character. There are also some stories in my life where I know I shouldn't be alive, and yet I stand. That is the power of God. When I thought all was lost, I would read the Bible and call on my

Higher Power, and my life changed so much that if the younger me were to see me right now, it would be like night and day.

Who do you call on when you feel lost, angry, overwhelmed, and stressed out? Imagine having someone who would never leave your side. That's how it feels when you open up to a spiritual vision. I remember when I was young and always looking to be rescued. Then I understood that no one was coming to rescue me, AND I didn't need to be rescued because God was already doing it. God is not a God of lack. My thoughts, feelings, and actions had to change to align with God's vision for my life. I had to renew in the Spirit, and because of my faith, I have been set free. I moved from hating to waiting on God's promises with an expectation of deliverance. I know that God's word shall never return to me void. When you have that level of faith, it produces different outcomes in your life. If you're wondering how this ties into self-love, it's loving yourself enough to find out the truth for yourself. Creating a spiritual vision is developing a plan to find out the truth. Reading, meditating, and journaling on the higher power of your choice is how it's done. When you educate yourself, that is freedom. No one can take that from you. Educating yourself is the ultimate act of love. No one can take your mind. You must be the one to free your mind from the chains that keep you in fear of what a human has done. Create a personal relationship with YOUR GOD!

Here are some journal questions to help you dig deeper. Writing the vision and making it plain will help you move forward in all areas of life. When creating your vision, you want to create SMART goals to track your success. SMART = Specific, Measurable, Attainable, Realistic and Time-bound. This can be a sensitive topic, so I suggest you take all the time you need; don't ever feel that you have to rush your healing. Take breaks and come back to the questions when you're ready.

***

I ask questions about your relationship with God because it's important to check your spiritual pulse. While digging deep into these questions, particularly as they pertain to people utilizing religion, you may find that some of your beliefs today are not actually yours or even God's desire for you. Instead, they could be handed-down beliefs hindering you from discovering what God has for you.

Question: What is the vision you have for your life?

_____
_____
_____
_____
_____
_____
_____

Question: How do you determine success?

_____
_____
_____
_____

___

___

___

___

Question: Do you have a personal relationship with God?

___

___

___

___

___

___

Question: Has anyone used religion to hurt you?

___

___

___

Tarnissha (Moe) Sass

_____
_____
_____
_____
_____

***

It's time to practice your mirror affirmations: Be sure to write them down and place them where you can see them often. You can use sticky notes or put them on the home screen of your phone. You want to be sure to speak them a minimum of three times daily.

Mirror Affirmations:

Affirm	Reaffirm
Nothing is impossible with my God.	I shall not fear.
My vision is clear.	I have everything I desire.
I am living to the fullest.	You are living your best life.
I celebrate each goal and success with gratitude.	You are celebrated, successful and grateful.
I am loved by my God.	You are loved by God.
God Chose Me.	You are God's favorite.

As simple as it sounds, we all must try to be the best person we can: by making the best choices, by making the most of the talents we've been given.
Mary Lou Retton

CHAPTER 6

Proper Preparation Prevents Poor Performance

God hasn't invited us into a disorderly, unkept life but into something holy and beautiful-as beautiful on the inside and the outside.

1 Thessalonians 4:7 (MSG)

If you want to set yourself up to win in life, it takes preparation. Preparation is key because nothing happens naturally, including unlearning all the toxic habits that brought you to a place of being disconnected. Preparation is also great because it allows you to take action and execute instead of standing around trying to make decisions. The more decisions you have to make, the more energy you use. When you set yourself up to achieve your goals ahead of time, the energy you would have expended making choices and decisions can be used to get stuff done.

Decision fatigue is real—it's the idea that after making many decisions, your ability to make more and more decisions during the course of a day worsens. The average person makes over 35,000 decisions a day. No wonder people are burnt out and exhausted. The way to combat this is by preparing and setting yourself up to win. Wouldn't you rather take one day to set up your week and then spend the rest of the week making fewer decisions? I know I do, and that's why I want to help you. Even while reading this book, it's not just reading. It's setting aside a time when you can concentrate and focus on yourself. I don't want this to be yet another book you read and toss to the side. I want you to read, meditate, reflect, and journal on each step.

Mindset will be the key to this lifestyle change of loving and choosing yourself. It starts from when you get up in the morning until you go to bed at night. So let's begin with how to prepare yourself mentally, emotionally, physically, nutritionally, and financially. First is your mindset. When you get up in the morning, you first want to thank your Higher Source for living another day. Gratitude will take you places that your money can't.

Here are some ways to win the week:

Pick either Saturday or Sunday and pick out your workout and work clothes for the week, down to your underwear and socks. When you take out the guesswork, you leave yourself with no excuses. If you have small children, pick out their clothes as well.

On the day you go grocery shopping, prepare your food for the week and place it in the fridge so you can grab and go. Or try a meal prep service. If you buy food using DoorDash, you can afford a healthy meal prep service such as Freshly, Splendid Spoon, Hungry Root or Blue Apron.

Either purchase a calendar or utilize the calendar on your smartphone to write out all appointments and reminders for the week. Schedule all doctor, dentist, chiropractor, massage and other self-love and care appointments, then put them on the calendar.

Here are some ways to win your morning:

Listen to something positive. You can listen while you're getting dressed AND in the car. If you commute to work, that's the perfect time to unplug from the mainstream radio or satellite and feed your mind something healthy and productive. There are many free channels on YouTube. Some of my favorites are Above Inspiration, Daily Motivation, Travis Eric, Inspiring Habit and Life Coaching w Sass. Take five minutes to read a scripture each morning from your Bible or something positive from a book of your choosing. Here are a few of my favorite scriptures from the book of Psalm (NIV Bible): Psalm 27:1, 37:4-5, 91:1-2, 139:14, 141:3-4, 141:8-9. Spiritual music is great to begin your morning because music invokes your soul to ignite. It moves you to all the beautiful places that are locked away inside you. It raises your vibration.

Have you ever listened to a song that sparked the most beautiful memory that lit you up inside? That's the beauty of music.

I use guided and unguided meditations. If you think you can't meditate, think again. It's just like learning multiplication. Repetition is mastery. Above all else, it allows you to connect with yourself on a deeper level. You don't have to just sit while meditating; you can incorporate shower meditations as well. This way, if you don't have time to sit or lay and meditate, you can still experience it. Here are some of my favorite YouTube meditation channels: Great Meditation, Brian Scott, Your Youniverse, Unlock Your Life, Black Minds Meditation and The Mindful Movement.

Write your intentions for the day and a list of items you will accomplish. This is an important step because it serves as a reminder and helps with intentional focus.

Exercising in the morning is a GREAT energy booster. If you can get in ten to 30 minutes of exercise, it boosts the serotonin levels in your brain, which affects your mood and overall well-being.

Now that we have some things you can do in the morning, here are some things you can do if you have an opportunity throughout the day:

Instead of scrolling on social media during your lunch break or anytime at work, listen to uplifting music, podcasts, sermons, or talks. It's important to keep the positive momentum going from the morning.

Take a healthy break and go for a walk while listening to something uplifting or funny. "A laugh a day keeps the doctor away" is one of my sayings. I find things to make me laugh to keep my spirit lifted, especially in the work environment. Some of my favorite people to listen to mid-day include Myles Munroe, Eric Thomas (ET the Hip Hop Preacher), Priscilla Shirer, Sarah Jakes Roberts, Motiversity, Jim Rohn, Rockstar Affirmations and Keion Henderson.

If at any point you feel anxious, overwhelmed or upset, try my 555 method. That's where I take 5 minutes to take 5 deep inhalations (be sure to expand your stomach), hold for a count of 5, then exhale and let it all out for an extended count of 5. The number 555 represents change, and when you incorporate breath work throughout your day, it will change your mood for the better.

Here are some great things to do in the evening:

Do a workout if you can't do it in the morning or during your lunch hour.

Do all your prep work for the next day, including placing your shoes, gym bag, kids' bookbags, and any items you need to put in the car at the front door.

While cooking dinner, prepare your food for the next day. I love the crockpot, especially if I didn't prep for the week.

Before bed, set your favorites on YouTube so you know what you're listening to in the morning. The goal is to remove anything that will stop you from achieving your goals. Before going to sleep, write your wins for the day. Most people reflect on what they didn't get done. That can be counterproductive. By the end of the day, I want you to see that you have won some things.

I do a sleep meditation to train my brain while I'm sleeping. I utilize YouTube for those as well. Some of my favorites are Brian Scott, Dauchsy and Good Vives Binaural Beats. Say a prayer of thanks to your higher source for helping you to get through another day. Prayer is an important part of preparation. Incorporate prayer, not to seek God's hand, but his face. In other words, don't just pray to gain something, but pray to give thanks for covering you and your family.

Reading this may make you feel overwhelmed, and this is why we prepare by developing a schedule.

Here is a sample of my schedule:

4:00 a.m. – 4:50 a.m.: Wake up, bathroom, meditation and prayer

4:55 a.m. – 5:00 a.m.: Put on workout clothes

5:00 a.m. – 5:55 a.m.: Journal, read the Bible, do my social media posts for my business

6:00 a.m. – 7:30 a.m.: Accountability call

7:30 a.m. – 8:00 a.m.: Insanity Max 30 workout

8:05 a.m. – 8:25 a.m.: Shower and get dressed

8:30 a.m. – 5:00 p.m.: Work (I work from home)

5:30 p.m. – 6:00 p.m.: Dinner

6:00 p.m. – 9:00 p.m.: Client meetings

9:00 p.m. – 10:00 p.m.: Set out clothes, shower, read, write and sleep

This is just a sample so you can see how to create time to get the maximum output. My schedule does change from time to time. I sneak in laughter throughout my day. Most of my leisure for right now is on the weekend.

***

Here are some reflection questions to get you thinking about how you can best prepare to take the time to care and fall in love with yourself.

Question: What do you need to say no to in order to say yes to adding items to your schedule that you love?

_____

_____

_____

_____

_____

_____

_____

_____

_____

Question: How can you set your schedule up so that you can take care of your mental, emotional, physical, nutritional, and spiritual needs?

_____

_____

_____

_____

_____

_____

Question: What can you delegate to give yourself more time in the day?

_____
_____
_____
_____
_____
_____
_____

***

It's time to practice your mirror affirmations: Be sure to write them down and place them where you can see them often. You can use sticky notes or put them on the home screen of your phone. You want to be sure to speak them a minimum of three times daily.

Mirror Affirmations:

Affirm	Reaffirm
I am organized.	You are organized.
I am brilliant.	You are full of brilliant ideas.
I have all I need to make today great.	Your day will be great.
I am getting better every day in every way.	You are better today.
I easily adjust to new situations.	You are adjusted.
I am prepared for the day.	You are prepared for the day.

*If you want to be respected for
your actions, then your behavior
must be above reproach.*
Rosa Parks

CHAPTER 7
Who Holds You Accountable?

He who walks with the wise grows wise,
but a companion of fools suffers harm.
Proverbs 13:20 (NIV)

We were not born to do life alone. One of the essential keys I found to staying on track in my journey was accountability. People who have a system of accountability in their lives transform into the best versions of themselves. Why is accountability important? Most of us live in our own minds and think from a right versus wrong mentality. While we are brilliant beings, we still have blind spots. Blind spots are places or spaces in our lives where we have good and bad habits and traits that are not visible to us but are visible to others. Even the most self-aware person is not aware of some of the traits and habits they display. When we eliminate our blind spots, it opens us up to be conscious of how we show up in the world.

When thinking of an accountability partner, think of someone who is truthful and holds you in high regard. A good accountability partner generally wants to see the best for you and doesn't operate in fear. When they hold you in high regard, they won't hold back on telling you the things that will help you step into your best life.

There are many ways to have an accountability partner, depending on what's going on at this point in your journey. I started off with a therapist because I knew if I didn't get help, I would continue to make the same mistakes in life and love. I was tired of failed relationships and friendships, and I was tired of feuding with myself. I knew it was time to face my childhood trauma and put in the hard work of healing. I had to face the hurt that I experienced and caused. I also had a life coach to keep me on track with my vision and goals. My coach helped keep me in alignment and to see the bigger picture of all that I wanted to accomplish. I joined many programs that also helped me be accountable for my healing and personal development. I did Emotional Intelligence Programs and Speaker Academies, and I still attend the program that hosts accountability calls at 6:00 every morning. The most important step was belonging to and creating my own community. Community helps keep you going on the days you want to give up. It's great to be your own cheerleader and imagine having others encouraging, pushing, loving and cheering you on. When you join the right community of like-minded positive individuals, that's what you'll experience. Community helps you understand that you are not alone nor do you have to be. Success is created in the individual but carried out with community.

If you're not sure of a community, life coach or therapist just yet but are serious about transformation and your self-love journey, you have to put the proper systems in place. If you have a friend who loves and supports you enough NOT to ride with your mess but push you to be your best, then use your friend. I found that it was better to have someone who didn't know me personally because they were not emotionally tied to me. People who are not emotionally tied to you, such as a coach, will challenge and push you outside your comfort zone. On the journey to loving yourself, comfort zones can't exist. You get to be comfortable with being uncomfortable. It may feel uncomfortable to learn how you have neglected and betrayed yourself by being a people pleaser and just wearing masks all your life to avoid people meeting the real you. Getting real requires help, and that is where an accountability partner can help you keep your commitments.

***

While reflecting on the questions below, I want you to think about acknowledging your fears. Acknowledging that fear is a learned behavior that will help you overcome it. If you can learn fear, you can unlearn it as well. An accountability partner can help you as you face those fears and can help bridge the gaps between where you are now and where you want to be. An accountability partner can also help shed light on the actions you are not taking to live your dream life.

Question: In what areas of your life are you unsatisfied?

_____

_____

_____

_____

_____

_____

_____

Question: Why are you not living the life of your dreams?

_____

_____

_____

_____

_____

_____

_____

_____

Question: Do you feel unworthy of your dreams, and if so, who made you feel that way?

_____

_____

_____

_____

_____

_____

***

There comes the point in your life where being independent will only get you so far. There will be a point in the journey where a soul tribe, which is a group of supportive individuals that resonate and share similar values, will help you along your journey. And having an accountability partner who's already at the point where you desire to grow to will be a game-changer in your life.

Surround yourself with the people who are already doing what you want to do, NOT the people trying to do it. If you want to know what the next five years of your life will look like, then look at the circle of people you hang around because that's exactly what it will be. If you're the smartest person in the room, you're in the wrong room. Instead, get around people who will stretch and push you outside your comfort zone because that's where the magic of life happens.

***

It's time to practice your mirror affirmations: Be sure to write them down and place them where you can see them often. You can use sticky notes or put them on the home screen of your phone. You want to be sure to speak them a minimum of three times daily

Mirror Affirmations:

Affirm	Reaffirm
I am accountable for my life.	You are accountable.
I am a magnet for blessings.	You are a magnet for blessings.
I am not my mistakes.	Your mistakes don't define you.
I forgive myself.	You are forgiven.
My possibilities are endless.	Everything is possible for me.
I love myself unconditionally.	You are loving.

Accountability separates the wishers in life from the action-takers that care enough about their future to account for their daily actions.
John Di Lemme

Conclusion

Glory be to God! By his mighty power at work within us, he is able to accomplish infinitely more than we would ever dare to ask or hope.
Ephesians 3:20 (NLT)

Taking accountability is the right thing to do. However, I had to learn that it takes two to create a situation in my life. Once I started to learn that there was nothing wrong with me—I was enough—I was just in the wrong places, with the wrong people, trying to fit, I learned to love me and find my way. I had to believe that I was enough. The principles I listed in this book were the catalyst to my success.

They helped me break free from all the past pain and trauma. I'm no longer the bag lady carrying around all her emotional baggage. I'm happy, vibrant, passionate, successful and learning more about myself every day. I love everything about the woman I am and becoming.

When I was at my worst, struggling to survive in a world that wants you to do everything except love and accept yourself, it was then that I realized I was my own worst enemy. And if I wanted my family to have and be better, I had to start with me. That's what finding your way is all about. The moment I realized that I didn't have to be a victim of my circumstances any longer was the day my life changed. My "enough was enough" moment happened resulted from years of pain and suffering in silence.

I want you to start with you. Take these principles and make them your own. The key is to just start. Small consistent changes every day will transform your life. Transformation happens when you change your core beliefs. I want you to believe that your path to wholeness begins with you loving yourself. I want you to know you can find your way. Just know that everything you desire is on the other side of deciding to take action with your mental, emotional, physical, nutritional and spiritual health.

If I could sum up one thing to take away from this book, it would be this: the day you say YES to yourself will be the day you create freedom for everyone around you. That just leaves me with some final questions because when you understand that you can be, do, or have anything in this world and begin to choose yourself, it won't just affect you but everyone who encounters you. Healed and whole people speak, live, and act differently.

***

When you say yes to your life, who will become free in your family and friends circle?

When you say yes to yourself, what generational curses will you break?

When you say yes to yourself, what generational blessings will you create?

Will you say YES to loving yourself?

Will you commit to taking action to find your way?

Affirm: I will find MY way. Reaffirm: My path to wholeness is clear.

Affirm: You are unstoppable every time you say YES to loving YOU. Reaffirm: YOU ARE UNSTOPPABLE!!!

*If you believe in a God who
controls the big things, you have to believe
in a God who controls the little things.
It is we, of course, to whom things look
"little" or "big."*
Elisabeth Elliot

Let's Connect

I would love to hear from you. Let me know what you think about the book, any questions, or join my community.

Website: www.moesass.com

Email: info@moesass.com

YouTube: youtube.com/@moesass

Facebook: Life Coaching w/ Sass

Instagram: Scan QR Code

When you subscribe to my email list, I'll send a powerful workbook I developed to help you at any stage of your journey to finding your way.

About the Author

Tarnissha Sass is an award-winning author, vision and empowerment coach, and speaker. She was born and raised in New Jersey. She is a proud mother of six children (five living) and two grandchildren. She has worked in Management at a Fortune 500 Company for the last 25 years. In addition, she lives out her purpose.

Before becoming a professional speaker with the National Speakers Association, certified Eric Thomas & Associates, LLC Speaker, and certified Vision and Empowerment Life Coach, Tarnissha was a fitness professional. Tarnissha is all things women's empowerment and enjoys working and teaching women to develop, grow and live the life of their dreams. She is faith-driven and gives God all the glory.

Tarnissha lives in Pennsylvania as an empty nester and is enjoying what she calls her New Testament of life.

www.ingramcontent.com/pod-product-compliance
Lightning Source LLC
LaVergne TN
LVHW021410080426
835508LV00020B/2542